L'ANGLAIS POUR LES ENFANTS

I SPEAK ENGLISH TOO! 2

I0181750

ISBN: 978-1-914911-12-5

www.zigzagenglish.co.uk

ZIGZAG ENGLISH

OUR BOOKS FOR CHILDREN
www.zigzagenglish.co.uk

Our bilingual books for young children. *Funny stories in simple, useful everyday English, with colour photos.*
English with Tony -1- Tony moves house
English with Tony -2- Tony is happy
English with Tony -3- Tony's Christmas
English with Tony -4- Tony's holiday
My Best Friend

Our coursebook for child beginners *(age 7 to 11)*
English for Children - 1st Coursebook (Essential vocabulary and grammar for beginners)

Our series of dialogue books for beginners *(for beginners aged 7 - 11). With word lists, comprehension questions, speaking tasks and more.*
I Speak English Too! - 1
I Speak English Too! - 2

Our series of reading and comprehension books for beginners *(for beginners aged 7 - 11). With word lists, comprehension questions and more.*
Read English with Zigzag - 1
Read English with Zigzag - 2
Read English with Zigzag - 3
Read English with Zigzag 1, 2 and 3
      Audiobook - Books 1 + 2 (Audible)

The Learn English Activity Book for Children *(A1 - A2, elementary). (Recommended for children in early secondary school.)*

Our series of reading and comprehension books for children at elementary level *(recommended for ages 10 - 13). With word lists, comprehension and discussion questions and lots of language activities.*
Read English with Ben - 1
Read English with Ben - 2
Read English with Ben – 3

Our series of reading and discussion books (with writing tasks) for children at secondary school, A2 - B1
I Live in a Castle – Book 1 – The Choice
I Live in a Castle – Book 2 – The New Me

The Speak English, Read English, Write English Activity Books – *3 books from A1 to B2, for older children and adults.*

Our non-fiction book with language activities
Learn English with Fun Facts! – A2 – B2

English Dialogues for Secondary School – for ages 11 to 17, A2 – B2

OUR BOOKS FOR ADULTS

Our 3 Grammar books with grammar-focused dialogues
Learn English Grammar through Conversation – A1, A2 and B1

Our Dialogue books for adults (with vocabulary lists and comprehension questions)
50 very Easy Everyday English Dialogues (A2)
50 Easy Everyday English Dialogues (A2 - B1)
50 Intermediate Everyday English Dialogues (B1 - B2)
50 more Intermediate Everyday English Dialogues (B1 - B2)
40 Advanced Everyday English Dialogues (B2 – C1)
40 Intermediate Business English Dialogues (B1 - B2)
40 Advanced Business English Dialogues (B2 - C1)

Our activity books for adults and older children
The Speak English, Read English, Write English Activity Books – 3 books, for A1 - A2, A2 - B1 and B1 – B2.

Our non-fiction book with language activities
Learn English with Fun Facts! – A2 – B2

Contents

Les objectifs de cette série de livres:
1. Donner à votre enfant plus de confiance pour lire et parler anglais.
2. Enseigner à votre enfant, de manière ludique, des mots et des phrases clés, qui seront ensuite utilisés pour l'aider à élargir son utilisation de l'anglais.

Notre méthode pour enseigner l'anglais aux enfants:
1. Ces livres ont été écrits par une enseignante d'anglais qualifiée et expérimentée. Ils ont été testés par des enfants d'âge primaire qui apprenaient l'anglais à partir de zéro.
2. Si vous parlez un peu d'anglais, vous pouvez utiliser ces livres pour aider votre enfant. Vous n'avez pas à vous inquiéter de faire des erreurs - vous pouvez simplement lire les phrases du livre. Mais si vous le souhaitez, vous pouvez aller plus loin en utilisant les dialogues pour avoir de nouvelles conversations avec votre enfant.
3. Les dialogues sont bien sûr parfaits pour les frères et sœurs aussi.
4. Les dialogues commencent au niveau A1 (atteint dans le livre 1) et ajoutent ensuite des mots et des phrases pour développer l'anglais de votre enfant. Il peut apprendre davantage grâce à des questions de compréhension, des "Remplir les Blancs" et des "Recherches de Mots".
5. En 23 dialogues, votre enfant passera de "Maybe your school is fun. My school isn't." à "I can't believe you think singing is better than playing football."
6. Il sera alors prêt à passer à des conversations encore plus complexes.

Comment utiliser ce livre:
1. Lisez le dialogue A avec votre enfant.
2. Regardez ensemble la liste de vocabulaire et aidez votre enfant avec les nouveaux mots.
3. Changez de rôles et lisez à nouveau le dialogue.
4. Encouragez votre enfant à faire l'exercice. L'exercice "Fill the Gaps" peut être fait sans se référer aux phrases originales - c'est un défi amusant. Ou, plus facilement, vous pouvez demander à votre enfant de regarder les phrases manquantes - elles se trouvent en bas de l'exercice - et de choisir les bonnes. Les

réponses aux <u>questions de compréhension</u> des dialogues 2, 4, 6, 8 et 10 se trouvent à la fin du livre.

5. Lisez le <u>dialogue B</u>. Changez de rôles et relisez-le.
6. Posez à votre enfant les questions à *C: What about you?*
7. Si vous le souhaitez, vous pouvez essayer une conversation avec votre enfant en utilisant le langage des dialogues A et B, ainsi que le langage des dialogues précédents. Vous pouvez bien sûr introduire de nouveaux mots et de nouvelles phrases. Selon nous, c'est la manière la plus efficace d'enseigner l'anglais à un enfant. Vous aiderez votre enfant à élargir son utilisation de l'anglais jour après jour.

Quoi d'autre? Et après?

1. Encouragez votre enfant à lire des livres, à écouter des livres audio et à regarder des émissions pour enfants en anglais facile. Pourquoi ne pas essayer notre série de livres pour enfants de niveau A1 à B1: **Read English with Zigzag**? C'est l'histoire d'un chat, d'un chien, d'un frère et d'une sœur. C'est drôle! Il y a beaucoup d'images! Les livres comprennent également des listes de vocabulaire anglais / français, des questions de compréhension et des activités linguistiques. Il y a aussi un **livre audio**.
2. C'est passionnant de voir son enfant faire des progrès rapides dans une nouvelle langue. Bonne lecture, et amusez-vous bien!

LESSON 1

1A: Why's it boring?

Anna: Are you **back** at school now, Katie?

Katie: Yes, I am. It's so boring!

Anna: Why's it boring?

Katie: I go to school every **morning**. I have **the same** teacher every day. I see the same friends. In the afternoon, I go home and do my homework. Of course it's boring.

Anna: School's not boring. It's quite **fun**.

Katie: Maybe your school is fun. My school isn't.

Anna: But you don't really go to school every day. You don't go to school on Saturday or Sunday, do you?

Katie: No, I don't go to school at the weekend. But I go to school on Monday, Tuesday, Wednesday, Thursday and Friday!

Anna: I like school. I like seeing my friends and **learning** new things.

Katie: You're right. School's not too bad. But **holidays** are better.

Anna: When's your next holiday?

Katie: In six **weeks**. **I can't wait**!

Vocabulary
- back   de retour
- morning   matin
- the same   le même
- fun   amusant
- to learn   apprendre
- holiday   vacances
- week   semaine
- wait   attendre
- I can't wait! j'ai hâte d'y être!

1A: Fill the gaps

Anna: Are you back at school now, Katie?

Katie:

Anna: Why's it boring?

Katie:

Anna: School's not boring. It's quite fun.

Katie:

Anna: But you don't really go to school every day. You don't go to school on Saturday or Sunday, do you?

Katie: No, I don't go to school at the weekend. But I go to school on Monday, Tuesday, Wednesday, Thursday and Friday!

Anna:

Katie: You're right. School's not too bad. But holidays are better.

Anna:

Katie: In six weeks. I can't wait!

1. Maybe your school is fun. My school isn't.
2. When's your next holiday?
3. I like school. I like seeing my friends and learning new things.
4. I go to school every morning. I have the same teacher every day. I see the same friends. In the afternoon, I go home and do my homework. Of course it's boring.
5. Yes, I am. It's so boring!

1B:

Sam: What do you do **after** school, Jack? Do you **just** go home?

Jack: Sometimes I go home. But sometimes I do sport.

Sam: What sport do you do?

Jack: I **play** football.

Sam: When?

Jack: I play football on Monday.

Sam: I play football too. But not on Monday, on Wednesday. Do you play football at school?

Jack: No, I play at a football club. Where do you play?

Sam: I play at school. And I often play at the park too, with friends.

Jack: I do judo too. I love judo.

Sam: I don't do judo, but I do karate. Karate's fun. I do karate on Thursday.

Jack: What do you do on Friday?

Sam: I'm **usually tired**, so I **watch television** with my family.

Vocabulary
- after   après
- just   juste, simplement
- to play   jouer

- usually   généralement
- tired   fatigué
- to watch television   regarder la television

1C: What about you?

1. *What's better – school or holidays?*
2. *What do you do after school?*
3. *What's your favourite sport?*

LESSON 2

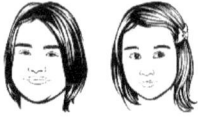

2A: What are you good at?

Anna: If you think school is boring, why don't you do **something** after school?

Katie: Like what?

Anna: Like sport, maybe?

Katie: I'm bad at sport. Are you good at it?

Anna: I'm **pretty good** at **swimming**. I'm in a swimming club.

Katie: How often do you go swimming? Every week?

Anna: I go swimming **twice** a week – on Tuesdays and Thursdays.

Katie: That's **too much** swimming. And I'm not very **good at** it.

Anna: So what ARE you good at?

Katie: I don't know. I quite like **singing**.

Anna: Why don't you **join** a **choir** then?

Katie: That's a good idea. Thanks, Anna!

Vocabulary
- something   quelque chose
- pretty good   plutôt bon
- to swim   nager
- twice   deux fois
- too much   trop
- good at   bon à
- to sing   chanter
- to join   rejoindre
- choir   chorale

2A: Find the right answer

1. What is Katie good at?
   - a. She's good at swimming.
   - b. She's good at singing.
   - c. She doesn't know what she's good at.

2. How often does Anna go swimming?
   - a. She goes swimming three times a week.
   - b. Twice a week.
   - c. Once a week

3. What is Katie bad at?
    a. She's bad at English.
    b. Singing.
    c. She's bad at sport.

2B:

Sam: **What's wrong**, Jack?

Jack: **Nothing**. Why?

Sam: I don't know. You don't look very **happy**.

Jack: I'm fine.

Sam: Really?

Jack: Okay, I'm not fine. My mum wants me to…

Sam: What?

Jack: My mum thinks I do too much sport.

Sam: Too much sport?!

Jack: Yes. She wants me **to stop** playing football.

Sam: That's bad.

Jack: Yes, I know. And that's not all. She wants me to…

Sam: What?

Jack: She wants me to **try** singing. She wants me to join a choir.

Sam: Oh no!

Vocabulary
- what's wrong?   qu'est-ce qui ne va pas?
- nothing   rien
- happy   heureux
- to stop   arrêter
- to try   essayer

2C: What about you?

1. *What are you good at?*
2. *What are you bad at?*
3. *Do you do too much sport?*

I

LESSON 3

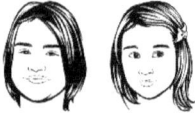

3A: Mum says I can

Anna: So how's school, Katie? Is it **still** boring?

Katie: Yes, it's still a bit boring.

Anna: What about after school?

Katie: That's a bit **more interesting**. My mum says I can join a choir!

Anna: Really? That's great!

Katie: Yes, it is, isn't it?

Anna: Is there a choir at your school?

Katie: No, there's not. There isn't a choir at my school, but there's a children's choir in Cambridge. It's for children from 8 to 13.

Anna: That's **perfect**.

Katie: Yes, it's **just right** for me.

Anna: When do you start?

Katie: **Next week**. I can't wait!

Anna: Let's **talk again** next week. I want to know **how it goes**.

Vocabulary

• still	encore
• more	plus
• interesting	intéressant
• perfect	parfait
• just right	parfait
• next week	la semaine prochaine
• to talk	parler
• again	encore
• how it goes	comment ça se passe

3A: Fill the gaps

Anna:

Katie: Yes, it's still a bit boring.

Anna:

Katie: That's a bit more interesting. My mum says I can join a choir!

Anna: Really? That's great!

Katie:

Anna:

Katie: No, there's not. There isn't a choir at my school, but there's a children's choir in Cambridge. It's for children from 8 to 13.

Anna:

Katie: Yes, it's just right for me.

Anna: When do you start?

Katie:

Anna: Let's talk again next week. I want to know how it goes.

1. Next week. I can't wait!
2. Is there a choir at your school?
3. That's perfect.
4. What about after school?
5. Yes, it is, isn't it?
6. So how's school, Katie? Is it still boring?

3B:

Jack: So how's football?

Sam: It's good, thanks. Are you still playing football?

Jack: No, I'm not. I can't play football **anymore**.

Sam: **I'm** really **sorry**.

Jack: I'm sorry too. I'm so **angry** with my mum. She knows I love football.

Sam: What does your dad **say**?

Jack: He thinks mum's right. He wants me to do **less** sport. He wants me to try singing.

Sam: Are you good at singing?

Jack: I don't know. Mum and dad think I am. That's why they want me to join a choir.

Sam: Is there a choir at your school?

Jack: There is a choir at school, but it's really bad. So my parents want me to join a choir in **town**.

Sam: What choir? What's its name?

Jack: It's called The City of Cambridge Children's Choir.

Sam: When do you start?

Jack: **Tomorrow**!

Vocabulary
- anymore   plus
- I'm sorry   je suis désolé
- angry   en colère
- to say   dire

- less   moins
- town   ville
- tomorrow   demain

3C: What about you?

1. *Do you sing in a choir?*
2. *How often do you play football?*
3. *Is there a choir at your school?*

LESSON 4

4A: Who wants to be different?

Katie: Is this where the children's choir is?

Jack: I don't know. **Probably**.

Katie: Are you new too?

Jack: Yes. I don't really want to be here.

Katie: Why not? I'm **excited**!

Jack: Singing's okay for girls, but **I'd rather** be at football.

Katie: My mum says there are lots of boys in the choir. And it's a chance to make some new friends.

Jack: I **already** have friends, thanks.

Katie: Why are you here, then?

Jack: Because of my mum. My dad, too. They want me to learn to sing.

Katie: They're right. Every boy I know plays football. Why not do something a bit different?

Jack: I like doing the same things as my friends. Who wants to be different?

Katie: I think trying different things is interesting. It's nearly seven o'clock. Where are all the **other** children?

Jack: Look – **over there**. That's where they are. Let's go.

Vocabulary
- different   différent
- probably   probablement
- excited   enthousiaste
- I'd rather   je préfère
- already   déjà
- other   autre
- over there   là-bas

4A: Find the right answer

1. Why doesn't Jack want to be at choir?
   a. Because he doesn't like girls.
   b. Because he'd rather be at football.
   c. Because he doesn't want to learn to sing.

2. How many boys are there in the choir?
   a. There are no boys in the choir.
   b. There are lots of boys in the choir.
   c. There are three or four boys in the choir.

3. Do Jack and Katie want to do something different?
   a. Jack does, but Katie doesn't. Jack likes trying new things.
   b. No. Katie wants to do the same things as her friends.
   c. Katie does, but Jack doesn't. Katie thinks it's interesting to try new things.

4B

Anna: Do you like the choir?

Katie: Yes, I think so. The singing is quite **hard, though**.

Anna: Are the other children all good singers?

Katie: They're not bad. It's a good choir.

Anna: How big is it?

Katie: It's very big. There are **almost** sixty children.

Anna: How many girls and how many boys?

Katie: There are **about** forty girls and twenty boys. That's because **so many** boys just want to play football.

Anna: It's the same here. Are the other children in the choir nice?

Katie: I don't know **yet**. There is one boy I like, though.

Anna: Really? Who's that?

Katie: He's called Jack. He's new, too, but he's a good singer. He's much **better than** me.

Vocabulary
- hard   difficile
- though   mais
- almost   presque
- about   environ
- so many   tant de
- yet   encore
- better than   meilleur que

4C: What about you?

1. *Do you think trying something new is boring or interesting?*
2. *Do you like the same things as your friends, or do you like different things?*
3. *Do the boys at your school like singing? Why? / Why not?*

LESSON 5

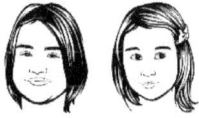

5A: A swimming race

Katie: So how are things in Paris?

Anna: Not bad. But I'm really **busy**.

Katie: Why?

Anna: I have a lot of work at school. The teachers give us lots of homework **now**.

Katie: **What about** your swimming? Are you still doing that?

Anna: Yes. I don't want to stop swimming. I like it a lot.

Katie: Are you in a **team**?

Anna: Yes. And we have a competition soon.

Katie: How many races are you in?

Anna: Just one **race**. I'm in the girls' **backstroke** race.

Katie: How far do you **have to** swim?

Anna: I have to swim 50 metres. And I have to swim very **fast**. It's **exhausting**.

Katie: When's the race?

Anna: It's in two weeks!

Katie: That's so **soon**. Are you excited?

Anna: I'm a bit **scared**. I don't want **to come last**!

Vocabulary

- busy   occupé
- now   maintenant
- what about   et …?
- team   équipe
- soon   bientôt
- race   course
- backstroke   dos crawlé
- to have to   devoir
- fast   vite
- exhausting   épuisant
- scared   effrayé
- last   dernier

5A: Fill the gaps

Katie: So how are things in Paris?

Anna: Not bad. But I'm really busy.
Katie: Why?

Anna:

Katie: What about your swimming? Are you still doing that?

Anna:

Katie: Are you in a team?

Anna: Yes. And we have a competition soon.

Katie:

Anna: Just one race. I'm in the girls' backstroke race.

Katie: How far do you have to swim?

Anna:

Katie:

Anna: It's in two weeks!

Katie: That's so soon. Are you excited?

Anna:

1. Yes. I don't want to stop swimming. I like it a lot.
2. How many races are you in?
3. When's the race?
4. I'm a bit scared. I don't want to come last!
5. I have a lot of work at school. The teachers give us lots of homework now.

6. I have to swim 50 metres. And I have to swim very fast. It's exhausting.

<u>5B:</u>

Sam: It's quite warm today. Do you think it's **spring** now?

Jack: I **hope** so. I hate cold **weather**.

Sam: What are you doing this weekend?

Jack: Nothing. Just homework. Why?

Sam: Do you want to play football?

Jack: Football? You know I don't play football now.

Sam: I know you don't play football at your football club. But can't you play with me and my friends? We play in the park. It's fun.

Jack: I don't know. What about my parents?

Sam: You don't have to **tell** them, do you?

Jack: Yes, okay. I really want to play some football. I **miss** it.

Sam: Good. **See you** on Saturday afternoon at the park.

Jack: Yes. See you!

Vocabulary
- spring   printemps
- to hope   espérer
- weather   temps
- to tell   dire
- to miss   manquer
- see you   à bientôt

5C: What about you?

1. *Are you in a team? What team are you in?*
2. *Do your teachers give you lots of homework?*
3. *Do you hate cold weather or hot weather?*

LESSON 6

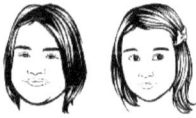

6A: I'm so tired

Katie: Are you having a good week, Anna?

Anna: Not bad. I'm busy. I'm swimming every day at the moment.

Katie: Every day? Don't you go swimming twice a week?

Anna: I usually go swimming twice a week, but it's the swimming competition next week, so I have to do more training.

Katie: When do you go swimming? In the morning or in the afternoon? **Before** school or after school?

Anna: I usually go swimming after school. But sometimes I go swimming at **lunchtime**.

Katie: Do you have **time** to go swimming *and* have lunch?

Anna: No, not really. When I go swimming at lunchtime, my mum **makes** me a sandwich. Sometimes I buy some chocolate, too.

Katie: You're **working so hard!**

Anna: Yes, it's really **tiring**. I have to go to bed early because I'm so tired. But I can **relax** after the competition.

Katie: When is the competition? Is it at the weekend?

Anna: No, it's next Thursday **evening**.

Katie: I have to go now – mum says it's dinner time. Good luck in the competition, Anna!

Anna: Thanks!

Vocabulary
- before   avant
- lunchtime   l'heure du déjeuner
- time   temps
- to make   faire
- to buy   acheter
- to work hard   travailler dur
- tiring   fatiguant
- relax   se détendre
- evening   soir

6A: Answer the questions

1. How often does Anna usually go swimming, and how often is she going swimming at the moment?
2. Does she go swimming before school?
3. What does Anna want to do after the swimming competition?

6B:

Jack: Hi, Sam. Where are your friends?

Sam: Thanks for coming, Jack. My friends are over there, **under** the **tree**.

Jack: Are they all boys?

Sam: No, there are two or three girls. Lots of my friends are girls, but they don't all play football.

Jack: Are they waiting for us?

Sam: I think so. It's half past three – time to play football.

Jack: Is your best friend here?

Sam: Yes. Daniel's the boy who's **kicking** the ball. He wants to start playing!

Jack: Is it **his** ball?

Sam: Yes, he always **brings** the ball.

Jack: Are your friends all good at football?

Sam: Some of them are very good at football. But some of them don't play very often, so they're not very good at it. **It doesn't matter**. We're just playing for fun.

Jack: You're right. Not **everything** has to be a competition.

Vocabulary
- under   sous
- tree   arbre
- to kick   frapper, donner un coup de pied
- his   son
- to bring   apporter
- it doesn't matter   ça n'a pas d'importance
- everything   tout

6C: What about you?

1. *Do you play football? Where do you play it?*
2. *Do you have a football? Where is it?*
3. *How many of your friends are boys, and how many are girls?*

Word Search 1

```
Q J S N H Z J H Y Q A X O T M
V S Q I U O R F U E E C M O B
W H P V S I H O L I D A Y M T
I X P T U V D A T R O R L O H
I Q S C A R E D C X T F H R W
V W F O L L U Y N Z J V S R E
G P G Y L W U F N X N F M O T
U E K U Y E X C I T E D K W V
P A W M A A J P R O B A B L Y
T I R E D T B E T T E R H F K
W I B G S H F R V S D B A B V
I Y Z A T E Z F H R S V R Q P
C O S P O R G E R H T O D W T
E K W M Q V Z C R A R D J Y L
W P H X F J R T J T T N N C Q
```

- I'm so **ex_i_ed**! I'm going on **h_l_d_y to_o_r_w**!
- What's the **we_th_r** like in the summer? It's **us_al_y** too hot.
- What's **b_tt_r** than coming second? Coming first!
- You look really **t_red**. You're **pro_a_ly** working too **_ar_**.
- It's the swimming competition tomorrow. I'm **sc_r_d**!
- I love my new school. It's **p_rf_ct**!
- I'm in a football club. I play football **tw_c_** a week.

LESSON 7

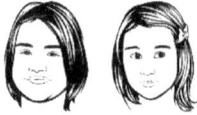

7A: A history lesson

Katie: So how did the competition go, Anna? Did you win?

Anna: No, I didn't. I didn't **win**, and I didn't come second, **either**. But I came third. I'm happy with that. Coming third is much, much better than coming last.

Katie: That's a great **result**. **Well done**!

Anna: Thanks. I can relax now. It's nice not to have to go swimming every day. What about you? How is school going?

Katie: It's going okay. I'm **enjoying history lessons at the moment**. History isn't usually very interesting, but we're learning some really interesting things at the moment.

Anna: Like what?

Katie: We're **learning about** Guy Fawkes.

Anna: What's that?

Katie: It's a man's name. He's **famous** in the UK.

Anna: Why is he famous?

Katie: He's famous for trying **to kill** the king. It's because of him that we all **celebrate** on the fifth of November.

Anna: What **kind** of celebration is it?

Katie: We usually have a big **bonfire**, with **fireworks**.

Anna: That sounds fun. I love fireworks.

Katie: Me too. My mum thinks they're **dangerous**, but my dad always buys some for Bonfire **Night**.

Anna: Bonfire Night?

Katie: The fifth of November, **remember**?

Vocabulary

• to win	gagner
• either	non plus
• result	résultat
• well done	bien fait
• to enjoy	aimer bien
• history	l'histoire
• lesson	leçon
• at the moment	en ce moment
• to learn about	étudier
• famous	célèbre
• to kill	tuer
• to celebrate	célébrer

- kind   genre
- bonfire   feu de joie
- firework   feu d'artifice
- dangerous   dangereux
- night   nuit
- remember   se souvenir

7A: Fill the gaps

Katie:

Anna: No, I didn't. I didn't win, and I didn't come second, either. But I came third. I'm happy with that. Coming third is much, much better than coming last.

Katie:

Anna: Thanks. I can relax now. It's nice not to have to go swimming every day. What about you? How is school going?

Katie: It's going okay. I'm enjoying history lessons at the moment. History isn't usually very interesting, but we're learning some really interesting things at the moment.

Anna:

Katie: We're learning about Guy Fawkes.

Anna: What's that?

Katie:

Anna: Why is he famous?

Katie: He's famous for trying to kill the king. It's because of him that we all celebrate on the fifth of November.

Anna: What kind of celebration is it?

Katie:

Anna:

Katie: Me too. My mum thinks they're dangerous, but my dad always buys some for Bonfire Night.

Anna: Bonfire Night?

Katie:

1. That's a great result. Well done!
2. It's a man's name. He's famous in the UK.
3. The fifth of November, remember?
4. Like what?
5. So how did the competition go, Anna? Did you win?
6. That sounds fun. I love fireworks.
7. We usually have a big bonfire, with fireworks.

7B:

Sam: What are you doing this weekend, Jack?

Jack: I don't know. Probably not much. My mum and dad are working this weekend, so I can do what I want.

Sam: So can you just sit on the sofa, watch television and play **computer games** all weekend?

Jack: I **need** to do some homework. And I'm reading some manga.

Sam: I like manga, too. Can you **draw** manga?

Jack: No, I don't know how to. Why, can you?

Sam: A bit. It's not too hard. Lots of my friends draw manga. I usually draw manga at the weekend.

Jack: I'm not very good at art, but I like **writing.** I'm writing a **song**.

Sam: A song? What do you **mean**?

Jack: I'm writing a new song for my choir.

Vocabulary
- computer game   jeu d'ordinateur
- to need   devoir
- to draw   dessiner
- to write   écrire
- song   chanson
- to mean   vouloir dire

7C: What about you?

1. *What's your favourite celebration?*
2. *Do you sometimes play computer games all weekend?*
3. *Do you think drawing manga is hard?*

LESSON 8

8A: A week's holiday

Katie: It's my **half term holiday** next week. **A whole** week with no school!

Anna: Are you **going away**?

Katie: Yes. We're going to the Lake District.

Anna: What's that? Where is it?

Katie: It's in the **north** of England. There are lots of **mountains** and **lakes**. It's very beautiful.

Anna: Lucky you! I have school next week.

Katie: School is really hard at the moment. I'm tired. I need a **break**.

Anna: Is your whole family going?

Katie: No. My mum has to work next week. So she's **staying** at home.

Anna: Your **poor** mum.

Katie: **She doesn't mind** too much. She says she wants to have a nice **quiet** week with lots of television. And she wants **to go out** with some friends.

Anna: Does your mum have lots of friends?

Katie: Yes, she's really **popular**. But she's usually too busy to go out with them very often. She says that next week is a chance to have some "me time".

Anna: What does "me time" mean?

Katie: It means she **only** has to think about **herself**. No children or **husband** to **worry** about!

Vocabulary
- half term (holiday)   vacances de mi-trimestre
- whole   entier
- to go away   partir
- north   nord
- mountain   montagne
- lake   lac
- break   pause
- to stay   rester
- poor   pauvre
- she doesn't mind   ça ne la dérange pas
- quiet   tranquille
- to go out   sortir
- popular   populaire
- only   seulement
- herself   elle-même
- husband   mari
- to worry   s'inquiéter

8A: Answer the questions

1. Where's the Lake District?
2. Why isn't Katie's mum going on holiday?
3. Why doesn't Katie's mum have time to see her friends very often?

8B:

Sam: So how's your half term going?

Jack: We're not going away this time, so it's a bit boring.

Sam: We're not going away either. Well, we are, but only for three days.

Jack: Where are you going?

Sam: **Nowhere** exciting. Just to my grandparents' house.

Jack: Where do they live? **Somewhere** nice?

Sam: They live in London. It's not far. I like going to London. There's so much to see and do there.

Jack: Yes, London's really exciting. But my dad says it's too expensive. So we don't go there very often.

Sam: I'm lucky my grandparents live there. So it's cheap for us. They usually **pay** for everything.

Jack: What's your favourite thing to do in London?

Sam: I don't know. Probably the London **Dungeon**.

Jack: Why is it your favourite?

Sam: Because it's **dark** and very **scary**. It's fun!

Vocabulary

- nowhere   nulle part
- somewhere   quelque part
- to pay   payer
- dungeon   donjon
- dark   sombre
- scary   effrayant

8C: What about you?

1. *Where do you like going on holiday?*
2. *How busy is your mum?*
3. *How often do you go to Paris? Or do you live in Paris?*

LESSON 9

9A: It's spring

Anna: Did you have a nice holiday?

Katie: Yes and no.

Anna: What do you mean?

Katie: The Lake District is lovely. But there's not very much to do there, if you don't like walking.

Anna: Don't you like walking?

Katie: Not walking up enormous mountains, no! There are lakes, too, but you can't swim in them in February – the **water**'s too cold.

Anna: So are you happy to be back at school?

Katie: Happy to be at school? That's very **funny**. We're getting so much homework.

Anna: **At least** it's spring now. What's spring like in Cambridge?

Katie: It's lovely here now. It's not too cold, and there are **flowers everywhere**.

Anna: What do you like **best**, spring or **summer**?

Katie: Spring, I think. It's not too hot, and there aren't too many **tourists**.

Anna: I know what you mean. We get **loads** of tourists in Paris too!

Vocabulary
- water   eau
- funny   drôle
- at least   au moins
- flower   fleur
- everywhere   partout
- best   meilleur
- summer   été
- tourist   touriste
- loads   plein

9A: Fill the gaps

Anna:

Katie: Yes and no.

Anna:

Katie: The Lake District is lovely. But there's not very much to do there, if you don't like walking.

Anna:

Katie: Not walking up enormous mountains, no! There are lakes, too, but you can't swim in them in February – the water's too cold.

Anna: So are you happy to be back at school?

Katie:

Anna: At least it's spring now. What's spring like in Cambridge?

Katie:

Anna:

Katie: Spring, I think. It's not too hot, and there aren't too many tourists.

Anna:

1. It's lovely here now. It's not too cold, and there are flowers everywhere.
2. What do you mean?
3. Don't you like walking?
4. Happy to be at school? That's very funny. We're getting so much homework.
5. Did you have a nice holiday?
6. I know what you mean. We get loads of tourists in Paris too!
7. What do you like best, spring or summer?

Sam: Do you know what day it is tomorrow?

Jack: Umm…, Tuesday?

Sam: It's **Pancake** Day! My school is having a pancake race.

Jack: You mean when you have to run and **toss** a pancake with your **frying pan** at the same time?

Sam: Yes. It's good fun.

Jack: Are you any good at tossing pancakes?

Sam: They don't **use real** pancakes. They use tortillas. Tossing a tortilla is **easier than** tossing a pancake.

Jack: That's **cheating**!

Sam: **I suppose so**. But after school I make pancakes with my mum, so I toss those.

Jack: What do you put on your pancakes? **Lemon juice** and **sugar**?

Sam: Or chocolate sauce with bananas and ice cream.

Jack: That sounds **amazing**!

Vocabulary

- to toss   faire sauter
- frying pan   poêle, sauteusel
- to use   utiliser
- real   vrai
- easier than   plus facile que
- to cheat   tricher
- I suppose so   je suppose que oui
- lemon juice   jus de citron
- sugar   sucre
- amazing   incroyable

9C: What about you?

1. *What day is it tomorrow?*
2. *What do you put on YOUR pancakes?*
3. *Do you like spring or summer best? Why?*

LESSON 10

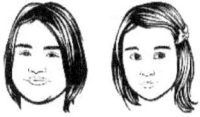

10A: A sleepover

Anna: I'm sorry you don't live in Paris, Katie.

Katie: I'm sorry, too. Paris is much more exciting than Cambridge. But why are you sorry I don't live in Paris?

Anna: Because you're so far away. I'm having a **sleepover** tomorrow, but of course you can't come.

Katie: That's really **unfair**. I never see you, and I love sleepovers.

Anna: Me too. Sara's coming, and two other friends. We're watching a scary film and my mum's making an enormous pizza.

Katie: That sounds great. You know, Anna, you can come and stay with me in Cambridge whenever you want.

Anna: What do you mean? For a holiday?

Katie: Yes. Why not?

Anna: What does your mum say?

Katie: My parents love having **visitors**. **Especially people** from other **countries**. They say it's interesting.

Anna: And my parents always want me to speak English.

Katie: When you come and stay with me, you can speak English all day, every day!

Vocabulary
- sleepover   pyjama party
- unfair   injuste
- visitor   visiteur
- especially   surtout
- people   personnes
- country   pays

10A: Answer the questions

1. Why do Katie's parents love having visitors from other countries?
2. Why can't Katie go to Anna's sleepover?
3. What does Katie want Anna to do?

10B:

Jack: I have a maths test tomorrow.

Sam: So?

Jack: It's a really important one.

Sam: Aren't you good at maths?

Jack: No, not really. I'm a bit worried.

Sam: Tests are scary. But if you do badly, it doesn't really matter.

Jack: What do you mean, it doesn't matter?

Sam: I mean, the school can't **punish** you.

Jack: The school can't punish me, but my parents can!

Sam: Do your parents punish you if you do badly at school?

Jack: Not usually. But maths tests are important.

Sam: Why are they so important?

Jack: Because my parents want me to go to **private school** when I **finish primary school**. But I can only go if I'm really good at maths and English.

Sam: I'm just going to the **secondary school** near my house. **Anyone** who lives near the school can go there. And my parents don't have to pay!

Vocabulary

- anyone   jeder
- to punish   punir
- private school   école privée
- to finish   terminer
- primary school   école primaire
- secondary school   école secondaire
- anyone   toute personne

10C: What about you?

1. *Do you think sleepovers are popular in your country?*
2. *How good are you at maths?*
3. *Do you enjoy tests, or do you think they're scary?*

LESSON 11

11A: A concert

Katie: I want to tell you something.

Anna: What?

Katie: I'm in a concert next week.

Anna: What kind of concert?

Katie: A choir concert. It's my first choir concert.

Anna: Are you excited?

Katie: I think I am. It's pretty exciting. We all have to wear the same clothes – black skirts or trousers and blue tops.

Anna: And what are you singing?

Katie: All kinds of songs. Pop songs, jazz songs and **classical** songs.

Anna: Is the boy you like still in the choir? Is he singing in the concert too?

Katie: Jack? Yes, of course he is. He's a fantastic singer now. He's singing a solo.

Anna: Is **everyone** in your family going to the concert?

Katie: My sister doesn't want to go, but mum says she has to.

Anna: Well, good luck in the concert!

Katie: Thanks!

Vocabulary
- classical   classique
- everyone   tout le monde

11A: Fill the gaps

Katie: I want to tell you something.

Anna:

Katie: I'm in a concert next week.

Anna:

Katie: A choir concert. It's my first choir concert.

Anna: Are you excited?

Katie: I think I am. It's pretty exciting. We all have to wear the same clothes – black skirts or trousers and blue tops.

Anna:

Katie: All kinds of songs. Pop songs, jazz songs and classical songs.

Anna: Is the boy you like still in the choir? Is he singing in the concert too?

Katie:

Anna: Is everyone in your family going to the concert?

Katie:

Anna:

Katie: Thanks!

1. And what are you singing?
2. Well, good luck in the concert!
3. Jack? Yes, of course he is. He's a fantastic singer now. He's singing a solo.
4. What kind of concert?
5. My sister doesn't want to go, but mum says she has to.
6. What?

11B:

Jack: Now the maths test is over, I can think about something nicer.

Sam: **Like** what?

Jack: Like the concert tomorrow.

Sam: What? You're in a concert?

Jack: Yes. I'm singing in a concert with my choir.

Sam: So you're still in the choir, then?

Jack: Yes, why not? I love the choir. It's better than judo. It's even better than football!

Sam: I can't believe you think singing is better than playing football.

Jack: Singing with fifty other people is lots of fun; and I love the **music**.

Sam: The good thing is, if you're singing with fifty other people, no-one can **hear** you if you make a **mistake**.

Jack: They can if you sing a solo.

Sam: But solos are for the really good singers.

Jack: Well, I'm singing a solo tomorrow night.

Vocabulary

- like   comme
- music   musique
- to hear   entendre
- mistake   erreur

11C: What about you?

1. *How often do you go to concerts?*
2. *What kind of music do you like?*
3. *Do you think singing a solo is scary or fun?*

LESSON 12

12A: I'm so happy

Jack: Where is everyone? Is this the right **place**?

Katie: I think so. What time is it?

Jack: It's a quarter to seven. Are we too early?

Katie: The concert starts at eight o'clock. So yes, we probably are too early.

Jack: How many people are coming to hear you sing?

Katie: My family. That's three people.

Jack: Lots of people are coming to hear me. My parents, my grandparents, my **uncle** and **aunt** and two cousins. I think **a few** of my friends are coming too.

Katie: That's because you're singing a solo.

Jack: Yes, I know. I'm **feeling** really **nervous**.

Katie: You don't need to worry. You're so good at singing.

Jack: Thanks. I'm so happy I'm in the choir.

Katie: So am I. And maybe if I work hard I can sing a solo **next time**.

Vocabulary
- place   endroit
- uncle   oncle
- aunt   tante
- a few   quelques-uns
- to feel   se sentir
- nervous   nerveux
- next time   la prochaine fois

12B: What about you?

1. *Do you want to join a choir?*
2. *How many cousins do you have? Are they girls or boys?*
3. *When do you feel nervous?*

Word Search 2

```
G M U O B C Q U I E T C N V F
Q P U C H M B W U V W O E N U
V T N W E Z W E I T G U Z V N
F C C R I I P D M V F N A Z N
U K D A E X P V K T G T R W Y
C Q R I W O D C M G Y R T D N
O O K J X F A M O U S Y I W F
C H E A P I N F M A H O I K Z
V I V M O R G Z M F Z L E Y Q
X N O A P E E L K X R I B L W
A V Y Z U W R V R X E Q B I A
F S M I L O O K Q S C A R Y T
X D B N A R U I O Y F Z R Y C
R Q B G R K S Q J X Z J O U H
E X P E N S I V E N X E U I V
```

- On Bonfire Night, we always **w_tch** the **f_r_w_rks**. They're **am_z_ng**. But it's a bit **_c_ry**, because my dad says they're **d_ng_r_us**.
- I want to buy this jacket. But is it **_hea_** or **_xp_ns_v_**?
- My best friend is a very **qu_et** girl. But she's quite **p_p_l_r**. She has lots of friends.
- Guy Fawkes is **f_mou_** in the UK because he tried to kill the king. Who is **f_mou_** in your **co_n_ry**?
- I like my teacher. He's so 😁 !

Réponses:

Dialogue 2A: Find the right answer

1: c
2: b
3: c

Dialogue 4A: Find the right answer

1: b
2: b
3: c

Dialogue 6A: Answer the questions

1: She usually goes swimming twice a week, but at the moment she's going swimming every day.
2: No, she doesn't. She goes swimming after school and at lunchtime.
3: She wants to relax.

Dialogue 8A Answer the questions

1: It's in the north of England.
2: Because she has to work.
3: Because she's usually too busy.

Dialogue 10A: Answer the questions

1: Because they think it's interesting.
2: Because Katie lives too far away. She lives in England and Anna lives in France.
3: Katie wants Anna to stay with her, for a holiday.

```
Q J S N H Z J H Y Q A X O T M
V S Q I U O R F U E E C M O B
W H P V S I H O L I D A Y M T
I X P T U V D A T R O R L O H
I Q S C A R E D C X T F H R W
V W F O L L U Y N Z J V S R E
G P G Y L W U F N X N F M O T
U E K U Y E X C I T E D K W V
P A W M A A J P R O B A B L Y
T I R E D T B E T T E R H F K
W I B G S H F R V S D B A B V
I Y Z A T E Z F H R S V R Q P
C O S P O R G E R H T O D W T
E K W M Q V Z C R A R D J Y L
W P H X F J R T J T T N N C Q
```

```
G M U O B C Q U I E T C N V F
Q P U C H M B W U V W O E N U
V T N W E Z W E I T G U Z V N
F C C R I I P D M V F N A Z N
U K D A E X P V K T G T R W Y
C Q R I W O D C M G Y R T D N
O O K J X F A M O U S Y I W F
C H E A P I N F M A H O I K Z
V I V M O R G Z M F Z L E Y Q
X N O A P E E L K X R I B L W
A V Y Z U W R V R X E Q B I A
F S M I L O O K Q S C A R Y T
X D B N A R U I O Y F Z R Y C
R Q B G R K S Q J X Z J O U H
E X P E N S I V E N X E U I V
```

Merci d'avoir lu ce livre!

Si vous avez des questions ou des suggestions pour améliorer le livre, vous pouvez m'envoyer un courriel à l'adresse suivante: lydiawinter.zigzagenglish@gmail.com. Les suggestions pour de nouveaux livres sont toujours les bienvenues.

Vous trouverez le site web de Zigzag English ici: **www.zigzagenglish.co.uk**. Votre enfant et vous pouvez découvrir nos autres livres pour enfants et adultes, lire le blog et faire d'autres activités en anglais.

N'hésitez pas à laisser un avis pour ce livre. Merci beaucoup!

Dans les pages suivantes, vous trouverez des extraits d'autres livres destinés aux enfants de niveau débutant à élémentaire.

11 I'm not scared

Are you there? Are you coming with me?

Be **careful**! Be careful of the cars!

Quick – **cross** the road now!

Where's Poppy? There she is. She's with Jessica.

But who are all the **other** people? There are so **many** people here. And so many cars and bikes.

Are you **scared**? Don't be scared.

I'm not scared. I'm **never** scared.

WHAT'S THAT?! IS IT A VERY BIG DOG?!

RUN!!

From: The Learn English Activity Book for children

MARK'S HOLIDAYS – True or False?

My name's Mark. There are five of us in my family – my parents, my older sister, my little brother and me. We live in a big, noisy **modern** city. My parents work very hard at work and my sister and I work very hard at school. So we love going on holiday!

My family goes on holiday once or twice a year. We usually go in the summer, in August, because that's when the long school holidays are. And sometimes we go away at Christmas too, to stay with my grandparents in their big house in a different, nicer city.

I like going on holiday in the summer because it's hot. We often go to the seaside and it's warm enough to swim in the sea. But my mum doesn't really like going to the beach. She says it's too hot and too boring. She likes staying in old hotels in beautiful towns and cities. She loves good food and she wants to eat at a different restaurant every evening. My little brother is only three. He's not interested in restaurants. He usually wants to go to the park to play on the swings. My sister is sixteen now. She says she wants to go on holiday with her friends next year. My dad always has fun on holiday. He's happy not to be at work!

1. Mark is the youngest child in his family. **T / F**
2. His parents both like their jobs. **T / F**
3. They go on holiday every year. **T / F**
4. They all like doing the **same** things on holiday. **T / F**
5. Mark's grandparents don't live in the **countryside**. **T / F**
6. Mark's sister is lazy. **T / F**
7. Mark loves his city. **T / F**
8. Mark's mum doesn't want to go to the beach every summer.
   T / F
9. Everyone likes hot weather! **T / F**
10. Mark stays with his grandparents in their flat once a year.
    T / F

14. Present

The day after the last day of school was the first day of the summer holidays. But Ben didn't feel excited. He felt unhappy.

He **lay** on his bed in his bedroom with a book. But he didn't read the book. He thought about all those years at primary school. He thought about his friends.

His mum **called** him. "It's lunchtime, Ben! Come downstairs!"

Ben **sighed**. He went downstairs to the dining room. He **started** to say: "I'm not hungry, mum. I don't want any lunch." But then he stopped. What was that on the table? It was a **parcel.** Was it a **present**? For him?

46

www.ingramcontent.com/pod-product-compliance
Lightning Source LLC
LaVergne TN
LVHW051200080426
835508LV00021B/2724